NATURE SERIES

TREES

By
JACQUELINE SEYMOUR

Designed by
DAVID GIBBON

Produced by
TED SMART

COOMBE BOOKS

INTRODUCTION

A tree can be defined as a perennial woody plant, usually having a single stem, which can grow to a height of six metres or more. Trees do not form a group of closely related plants but belong to many different families. There are, however, two main groups: the conifers and the flowering or broadleaved trees. In general, conifers are evergreen, bearing leaves all the year round, while broadleaved trees growing in temperate regions are deciduous, shedding their leaves in autumn and spending the winter in a dormant state. There are few deciduous conifers–the best known are the larches–but there are many evergreen broadleaves which are mostly native to the tropics where there is warmth and water all the year round and the shedding of leaves is not necessary for survival. In temperate regions the roots of trees can absorb little water from cold or frozen soils; if large leaves were retained water loss from them would occur at a much greater rate than water uptake and the tree would die. The hard, narrow leaves of conifers restrict water loss and enable them to survive the cold. These tough leaves also help some species to exist in hot dry climates.

Even the most casual observer is aware of the fruits of trees, whether horse chestnuts, acorns, winged seeds of maple or elm, pine cones or yew berries, walnuts or apples. The striking flower 'candles' of the horse chestnut and the beauty of apple blossom are also familiar, but the flowers of pine, larch, oak and elm are less well known. This is because they are all small and inconspicuous and, as is usual in nature, there is good reason for this; or, more accurately, there is good reason why some flowers are particularly noticeable. The flower is the means of sexual reproduction and its structure is directly related to the way in which fertilisation takes place. Large brightly-coloured flowers attract insects (or bats or birds) to them with the result that the pollen produced by the male parts of the flower, the stamens, is inadvertently transferred by these creatures to the female parts of the flower. This process of pollination leads to the development of the seed. The conifers are entirely wind-pollinated and do not have flowers with showy petals. They do not even have what is known as a 'perfect' flower, that is one which has both male and female parts. The more primitive conifers bear male and female flowers on separate trees; all the others have quite distinct male and female flowers on the same tree. Most of the broadleaved trees have perfect flowers which, even so, may be small and easily missed, like those of the elm. Wind pollination is not very efficient and pollen has to be produced in vast quantities to ensure that a sufficient number of ovules are fertilised.

Trees do not flower until they have been growing for some years. This period may be as short as ten years for a quick-growing tree like the sycamore and as much as forty years for the oaks. Growth takes place at the tips of the twigs and branches in the same way as in any green plant, but there is also growth of the trunk and the branches themselves. Fresh tissue is laid down each year by a single layer of cells, the cambium, which lies beneath the protective bark. The woody cells inside this layer conduct water from the roots to the leaves. Most of this sap flow takes place in the outermost and newest ring of tissue although some does occur nearer the centre of the bole. In a mature tree the heartwood is dead, but this gives the plant strength and rigidity; the living part of the tree is the relatively thin cylinder just under the bark. In cooler regions where growth ceases for the winter the woody layer can be seen to be composed of a number of rings, each of which is the result of one season's growth. The demarcation between the end of one year's growth and the beginning of the next is obvious because the cells made in spring are large with thin walls but as growth slows down the cells become smaller with thicker walls. It is these so-called annual rings which are used to establish the ages of trees accurately and also to study climate in years gone by.

If allowed to grow unhampered any given species of tree will develop a characteristic shape. Each species has its own pattern of buds and leaves giving a kind of blueprint for growth which allows all the leaves to have their fair share of light. The shape will, however, be modified by unfavourable circumstances such as competition for light from other plants.

Trees are no longer of supreme economic importance; they are no longer essential for housing and shipping, fencing or fuel. In a world increasingly composed of concrete, fibreglass and stainless steel, there are good aesthetic reasons why trees should be understood and preserved as well as vital biological and ecological ones.

Left: Autumn colours in Ontario, Canada.

The Yew

The Common Yew is a long-lived evergreen found only in the northern hemisphere. In Britain it is undoubtedly the tree which lives to the greatest age; there are a number of specimens over 1000 years old and some of these are almost certainly a good deal older. The Yew is commonly found in parks and gardens, being particularly suitable for hedging and topiary, and is traditionally grown in English and Welsh churchyards. The variety known as the Irish Yew, which has erect branches, has been much used for this purpose *right*. The reason for the association of the Yew with churchyards is obscure and none of the theories advanced is convincing. Some say it is because the tree was venerated by the Druids; others that it was planted there to exorcise the Devil, to ensure animals did not browse its poisonous leaves and berries, or to shelter resting pall-bearers from the wind.

The male flowers *below* and the female flowers *bottom right* are borne on different trees. The male flowers, which are found on the undersides of the shoots, produce large clouds of pollen in early spring. Each shoot of a female tree bears one or two tiny greenish flowers; after they are fertilised the fleshy covering round the base of each seed swells up to form a bright red cup-shaped fruit *top left*. The bark of the Yew *bottom left* is smooth and dark purplish-brown in colour. It flakes away to leave dark red, brown or yellowish patches.

Giants

The Giant Sequoia *left* is the largest living thing in the world in terms of bulk; the biggest specimen is a tree named General Sherman which is about 83 metres tall with a girth of about 24 metres. The Giant Sequoia grows on the western slopes of the Sierra Nevada in California. Also known as the Big Tree, Mammoth Tree, Sierra Redwood and Wellingtonia, it is placed in the genus *Sequoiadendron*. The Coast or California Redwood is, confusingly, a member of the *Sequoia* genus. The foliage of the Giant Sequoia is scale-like but the Coast Redwood has needle-like, slightly prickly leaves *right*. The Coast Redwood is found in a distinctly different habitat, that of the northern Californian coastal fog belt. The tallest tree in the world, at over 110 metres, is a Coast Redwood which has been called Howard Libby. The Swamp or Bald Cypress is a deciduous conifer, a North American close relative of the Redwoods. When growing in water it is noted for producing structures called knees *below* which grow out of the water and may be a method of supplying the submerged roots with air.

Larches

Few conifers drop their leaves in winter. The Swamp Cypress is one, the Dawn Redwood *(Metasequoia)* is another; all the larches are also deciduous. The most common American larch is the Tamarack, which is found from Alaska through Canada to the northern United States. Tamaracks are typically found growing in swampy ground and are shown *below* in autumn, growing along a stream. The female flowers *left* give rise to attractive rose-like cones. Both male and female flowers appear on the same tree, the male flowers being smaller and less conspicuous than the female. The cones of the European Larch *bottom right* are often retained on the tree for as long as ten years, sometimes longer, after they have shed their seeds. Larch leaves grow in distinctive rosettes or whorls except for those on new shoots which appear singly. New leaves like those of the Tamarack *right* are an attractive pale green. They darken as the year progresses and eventually become a rich gold before leaf-fall in autumn. The picture *far right* is of European Larch twigs at this time.

Pines

The pine family is the biggest family of conifers and includes the spruces, cedars and larches as well as the true pines. There are about forty species of spruce. The trees are valued for their timber and are frequently grown in large plantations like this one in North America *left*. The remaining members of the pine family illustrated are all true pines of the genus *Pinus*, of which there are about 100 species. The leaves of these trees are relatively long and needle-like and are borne in clusters of two, three or five, each of which is held together at the base by a papery sheath. Pines have a more sprawling habit than the spire-like growth of the spruces. The Scots Pine, shown in flower *right*, is a common European species. The male flowers *far right* are coloured bright yellow by the ripening pollen. Female flowers *below* are pale pink at first, becoming darker and almost purple by midsummer. The cones do not mature until the following year. The long needles are carried in pairs and have a bluish tinge.

The Bristle-cone Pine from the

White Mountains in California *below* is the oldest living thing, older even than the Coast Redwoods, some of which are 2,000–3,000 years old. The oldest living Bristle-cone Pine is 4,900 years old. The trees live in conditions of chronic drought and are extremely sensitive to minute differences in rainfall; this results in a unique pattern of annual rings which can be matched with an identical pattern in other trees. Dead wood *left* does not rot in the desert atmosphere and using this scientists have assembled records going back 8,200 years.

The Ponderosa or Western Yellow Pine *far right* is a huge and important timber pine which comes from the Californian mountains. The Aleppo Pine, the resin of which is shown *right,* is a tree common in the Mediterranean region; the Lodgepole *bottom right* is found in the western United States. The long straight trunks of the latter were used for Indian teepees.

13

The Loblolly Pine *left* is a large and fast-growing tree from the south-eastern United States. The resin smells of turpentine, as do the crushed leaves of the Lace-bark Pine which comes from China. This is an extremely slow-growing tree with beautiful bark *far left*. The greenish-brown bark peels off to reveal white patches which gradually change colour on exposure to the air, giving a range of subtle shades including buff, green and reddish and purplish browns.

The White-bark Pine *below* and the Limber Pine *bottom right* are both trees of the North American mountains which have needles arranged in groups of five. The Dwarf Mountain Pine *top right*, which comes from the Alps and south-east Europe, is really more a bush than a tree. It is shown smothered in male flowers; new brown shoots are also visible.

Conifers are all Gymnosperms, plants whose seeds are not enclosed in an ovary. They are considered to be more primitive and to have evolved earlier than the Angiosperms, to which the rest of the trees in this book belong.

Poplars

The willow family consists of two main groups; the willows, genus *Salix* and the poplars and aspens, genus *Populus*. These broadleaved trees are all extremely fast-growing, tending to be short-lived, and nearly all have male and female flowers on separate trees. The seeds are adapted for wind dispersal, each having a tuft of white hairs which enables it to be blown along like thistledown. The European scene *below* shows poplars growing in a typically damp place, at a lakeside. The North American Quaking Aspens *left and right* are very tough trees which can survive both drought and flooding. They are noted for the way their leaves shake and tremble even when there is no detectable breeze. This quaking happens because the leaf stems are unusually long and set at right angles to the blade. A male catkin consists of about fifty separate flowers, each of which is a cup holding a number of stamens; these catkins are dark red at first becoming yellow as pollen is produced. The female catkins are rather larger than the male, but they carry a similar number of flowers which ripen to form seed pods which split in midsummer releasing the tiny seeds.

18

Willows

The Weeping Willow *right* is the most famous of all the willows. The original Weeping Willow came from China; those cultivated in the West are generally hybrids which have the wild species somewhere in their ancestry. Because of its weeping habit the tree is decorative and graceful throughout the year, whether covered in leaves or with its bare twigs exposed. The Crack Willow, shown in spring, summer and winter *left,* is also an attractive tree although unable to vie with the delicate beauty of the Weeping Willow's flowing branches. The Crack Willow is so called because the twigs snap off audibly if pulled or bent. The Goat Willow or Sallow forms a bushy tree which produces the furry pussy willow catkins that children like so much. The catkins of different sexes (borne on different trees) are very similar in appearance before maturity and are particularly noticeable because they appear on the tree before the leaves. The grey furriness of the male catkins *below* is eclipsed by yellow as the stamens ripen; the female catkins *far right* remain a bright silvery green.

Walnuts

The Common Walnut has a very long history of cultivation. The Romans introduced it to Europe but it originally came from Persia. It is valued both for its delicious nuts, which also yield a fine oil, and its beautiful timber, often used in making fine furniture. Besides having an extremely attractive grain the wood is tough and light, properties which make it sought after for the stocks of guns and rifles. There are about fifteen species of walnut, native to North and South America and Asia. The American Black Walnut is the most vigorous of them all and is considered to be the best for both ornament and timber. These young trees *left* have been planted in South Africa.

Male and female walnut flowers grow on the same tree, appearing before the leaves. The male flowers are carried on catkins; the female flower *right* consists of a green flask-shaped ovary topped by yellow styles. The fruit of the walnut *below* consists of a green fleshy husk which eventually withers and exposes the familiar hard, wrinkled, nut shell.

The Silver Birch

The Silver Birch *left* is a common tree of sandy heaths in Europe. Its delicate and fragile appearance does not hint at its toughness and ability to endure extremes of both heat and cold. The silvery bark of this tree is another of its charms. That of the young sapling is shiny reddish-brown but soon the typical silvery-white colour appears. This outer layer of bark peels off and is constantly replaced. As the tree ages it becomes more rugged with black, roughly diamond-shaped patches *below*. Yet again the male flowers are grouped into catkins, which are visible on the tree for most of the year. In winter they are pale purplish-brown; in spring they expand and lighten before shedding pollen. A male catkin and female flowers are shown *right*. The female flowers are on the right and to the bottom, the male catkin is larger and to the left of the picture. The seeds *far right* are tiny and enclosed in two wings which carry them through the air.

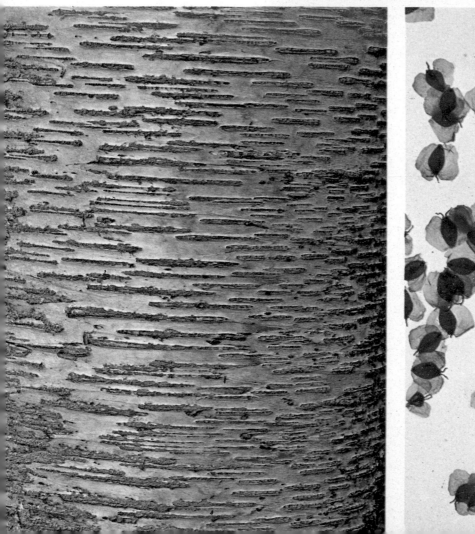

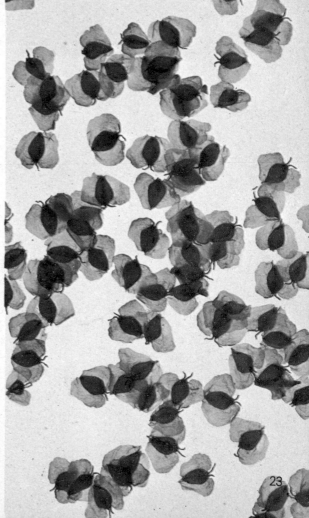

The Hazel

Hazels belong to the same family as the birches, alders and hornbeams. There are fifteen species of which only the Turkish Hazel always grows into a tree; the Common Hazel is a European species usually found growing as a shrub, but it will sometimes form a small tree. It has been important in forestry in the past, and was grown for poles used by cottagers for many things such as pea and bean sticks, fencing, firewood and wattles for wattle and daub house building. Now these uses have been largely superseded by other methods of heating, fencing and construction, and the Hazel is little cultivated for these purposes. Still commonly found in thickets and hedgerows, it has the largest and most familiar catkins of all *left*. These are sometimes known as lambs' tails to British children, or as Kätzchen or châtons to those in Germany and France. The tiny, hard, grey-green catkins can be seen on the bush in autumn *bottom right*. Each small female catkin *below* is composed of a number of flowers, each of which has two thread-like styles. The nuts *top right* grow in groups of up to four, each one being surrounded by a leaf-like frill. They provide food for many animals; cob nuts and filberts, varieties of hazel, are cultivated for human consumption.

The Beech

The seedleaves or cotyledons play an important part in the nourishment of many seeds. In some species they appear above the ground and make additional food material by photosynthesis. They bear no resemblance to the true leaves; the cotyledons of the Common Beech are strap-shaped *top far left*. The true leaves of this species open a few weeks later and are still tightly furled. The leaf buds of Beech *top left* are slender and pointed with sharp tips. Male and female catkins are separate but borne on the same twig *bottom far left*. The woody base round the female flower grows round the seeds to form a husk which encloses the sharply triangular nuts. An old seed case is shown *bottom left* with new leaves and a male catkin. The canopy of mature beech trees lets through little light, so preventing any undergrowth, except for plants like bluebells *right* which produce their leaves and make a food store before the light is blotted out. Beech leaves have attractive autumn colours. This is an avenue of beeches in autumn *below*.

The Oak

The English or Pedunculate Oak has held a special place in British history not least because it provided most of the timber used for building naval vessels. A mature tree *below* grows into a characteristically majestic shape, the crown being widely and irregularly domed and supported by a sturdy and massive trunk. This oak has leaves with very short stalks but the acorns *far right* are carried in pairs on long stems. In spring the young green leaves emerge from their buds *right* and the flowers appear. Male flowers *bottom right* are on very slender catkins which are grouped in bunches. Female catkins grow at the ends of new shoots. In the summer there is often further leaf growth; these leaves, shown here with a speckled bush-cricket, are red *left*.

Elms

The English Elm, a typical hedgerow tree *left*, is particularly subject to attack from bark beetles which, with their grubs, tunnel in the food-rich layers of the inner bark. This in itself would not normally be enough to cause a disastrous amount of damage, but the beetles are often infected with a fungus which invades the new ring of tissue just inside the cambium and blocks it, preventing most of the sap from rising from the roots and so killing the tree, as it has these *below*. In recent years the disease has spread rapidly through England, causing the death of thousands of trees. The elms are the first trees illustrated in this book which have perfect flowers; each flower has male and female parts, but there are no petals. The flowers of the English Elm *far right* and the Wych Elm *right* are very similar but the shape of the mature Wych Elm *bottom right* with its uniformly rounded head is very different from the waisted crown of the English Elm.

Figs

The Common Fig *left* is the only fig which will grow in temperate areas; it is a native of the Near East which grows well in a Mediterranean climate. The delicious fruits have well-known laxative properties and are used to make medicines. Tropical members of the Fig genus *(Ficus)* are often tall forest trees having buttressed roots *bottom right* which give the plant additional support. The banyan is a fig with aerial roots which have become greatly enlarged and spread away from the main stem, so acting, as far as support is concerned, like extra trunks. Some figs grow more like vines at first and twine among the forest trees. The roots of such a fig spread down the trunk of the host tree and thence into the ground; as they enlarge the host is gradually squeezed to death. Understandably they are called strangler figs; this one *top right,* also known as the Rock-splitting Fig, will have split the boulder completely in a few years' time. The fig leaf *below* was, according to the Bible, used by Adam and Eve to cover their nakedness. In Britain, during the era of Victorian prudery, tin fig leaves were fitted to statues in museums and other public places.

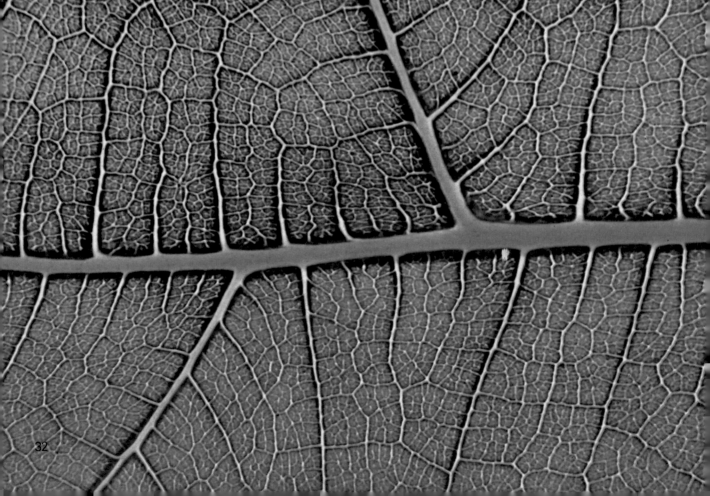

Magnolias

The magnolias are generally accepted to be among the most primitive of all the flowering plants. To the non-specialist this comes as a surprise because the large coloured flowers, composed of both male and female organs, seem more sophisticated than those of the broadleaved trees previously illustrated, most of which have small, distinct, male and female flowers and are wind pollinated. The magnolias, and their near relative the Tulip Tree, have enormous showy flowers. The fragrant blossom of the Japanese Big-leaf Magnolia *below* attract insects by both visual display and olfactory stimulation. The Tulip Tree has similarly large flowers *right* but the tree itself *left* is often so big that they are difficult to see clearly. Tulip Tree leaves are quite different from those of any other plant, being truncated at the tips to form saddle shapes. They become a rich bright yellow in autumn. In its native area, the eastern United States, the tree is known as White Wood, Tulip Poplar and Yellow Poplar. The timber is used for boat-building, furniture, boxes and pulp.

The Rose Family

The rose family is a large one containing plants of different sizes ranging from small ones like the wild strawberry and lady's mantle to shrubs like the bramble and raspberry and trees such as apple and cherry.

The Common Hawthorn never grows into a very large tree; it is perhaps more commonly seen as a shrubby growth in hedgerows. The berries or haws *left* are a popular food for birds; the seeds inside, protected by an indigestible bony core, can thus be carried some distance from the tree on which they grew. The tree *below* has been bent by the prevailing winds.

The Rowan or Mountain Ash *right* is not related to the Ash *(Fraxinus)*. It is a member of the same genus as the whitebeams and is similar to the hawthorn in having bright red berries which are dispersed by birds. The Rowan is also known as Quickbeam, White Ash, Witch-wood and Witchen and was formerly planted in Scottish glens for its supposed ability to protect against witchcraft.

37

Most of the common fruit trees belong to the rose family and of these the apple has probably been cultivated longer than any other. The Crab Apple is a tree of hedgerows and copses in its wild state and this tree, or something very like it, would have been the ancestor of our orchard apples. The Crab Apple *right* is cultivated nowadays for its beautiful blossom *below* rather than its small, hard, sour fruit, although this can be used to make an excellent jelly.

There are a large number of different varieties of cherry grown either for their large and profuse blossom or for their delicious fruit. All cherry bark has scattered horizontal scars on it, but the bark of some cherries is satiny, rather like that of birch. The Chinese or Tibetan Cherry is grown mainly for its beautiful bark *far left*. The European Wild Cherry or Gean *bottom left* is an attractively shaped tree which produces masses of white flowers in spring. This is the cherry whose wood was used for French furniture and whose fruits are used to make Kirsch liqueur.

The Almond is relatively hardy but the nuts do not ripen unless the climate is of the Mediterranean type. The fruit *left* is very similar to that of the peach but has a much thinner, not so juicy, layer of flesh.

Acacias

Acacias are members of the mimosa family and have the pea-like pods common to this family *left*. Africa is particularly rich in acacia species, some of which are typical savanna trees *right*; many of them have sharp-spined twigs and are known as thorn trees. In Australia and New Zealand, acacias are called wattles or sometimes mimosas. These *below* are growing in the central area of the North Island of New Zealand. The tiny individual flowers of the wattle are aggregated into pompoms which are in turn clustered together.

There are differing opinions on how the Rain Tree *below* got the reputation of being able to make rain. This could derive from the fact that in its native South America many cicadas feed in it so that anyone standing underneath is showered by a continuous rain of droplets ejected by them; alternatively it may be because, like some other mimosas, the leaves close up at night, so reducing water loss to the plant but also allowing rain to fall more readily to the ground beneath the tree resulting in lusher vegetation there than under other trees. The Rain Tree is also widely known as the Saman and Cow Tamarind; the seeds are used for cattle fodder.

Flowering Wood

The Judas Tree and the Cacao are not close relatives but they both have the unusual habit of producing flowers directly from the trunk. The Judas Tree flowers appear on the twigs and branches as well as the bole *left*, the leaves appearing after the first flowers. This plant is a member of the pea family and its pea-like pods are unusual because they do not split open to disperse the seeds but the entire pods are blown away by the wind. Popular legend has it that this is the tree on which Judas Iscariot hanged himself.

The Cacao is a member of the gum tragacanth family which also includes the cola or kola trees; the nuts of the latter are used in drugs and as flavouring for soft drinks. The powdered beans *right* of the Cacao tree are used to make cocoa and chocolate. Elaborate methods of insect pollination are the rule in this family; Cacao flowers *below* are pollinated by a large number of different small insects.

The Pea Family

There are no acacias native to Britain. The tree sometimes called the acacia in that country is the Black Locust or False Acacia *(Robinia)*. This ornamental tree has showers of fragrant flowers *above* which are similar to those of the Laburnum and are responsible for the alternative names of White Laburnum and Silver Chain. The Pagoda or Scholar's Tree from China has similar white pea flowers but its main attraction lies in the unusual shape of the contorted branches. The weeping variety 'Pendula' *left* rarely flowers. The Flamboyant Tree *right* is a tropical species also known as the Royal Poinciana, Flame Tree or Peacock Flower.

Erythrinas *left and below* are gaudy tropical or subtropical trees with bright red flowers which are often known as Coral Trees. The Siris or Woman's Tongue Tree *right* is grown as an ornamental away from its native areas of Asia and the Middle East. It has pods which grow up to thirty centimetres long. It is a member of the same genus as the Silk or "Mimosa" Tree which, in common with some acacias, has the unusual habit of folding its leaflets together in the evening, thus reducing water loss during the period of darkness when photosynthesis cannot take place. The Laburnum is commonly grown in parks and gardens in Europe but is rarely found if not deliberately planted. This may be because rabbits like the bark. If so, this is presumably not poisonous to them, but all parts of the tree are poisonous to us, the seeds in particular being dangerously emetic. The long pendulous bunches of flowers, seen from below *bottom right*, are its main attraction.

Hollies

The English Holly is a small evergreen tree with unmistakable shiny spiky leaves. These leaves vary a great deal in shape, different kinds being commonly found growing on the same tree. One of the most noticeable differences is that leaves near the bottom of the tree have long spines while those at the top lack spines altogether. The leaves have a waxy coating which reduces water loss; each individual leaf lives for only two or three years, most of the tree's annual leaf fall occurring in the spring. The common English Holly produces flowers of separate sexes, both of which have small white petals, carried on different trees. Male flowers and leaves are shown *right*; only a female tree will produce berries *left*. The leaves of the American Holly *below* have a thinner wax coating and are less glossy and more olive-green in colour.

Maples

The leaf of the Sugar Maple, the Canadian emblem, is the palmate shape typical of most species of Maple *(Acer)*, including the Sycamore. One of the most distinctive exceptions is the Box-elder or Ash-leaved Maple which has leaves with three to five separate leaflets, like those of the ashes. Another typical feature of the maples is their winged seeds or keys; the seeds, each of which has one wing, are paired at first, but usually split before whirling through the autumn air. These are the keys of Box-elder *above* and Sugar Maple *far left*. Maple sugar and maple syrup come from the Sugar Maple which is also noted for its striking autumn colouring but the very similar Red Maple *right* is even more spectacular. This tree, also known as the Swamp or Water Maple, for obvious reasons, is beautifully coloured all the year round, having glossy red twigs, small red flowers and red keys. The Norway Maple occasionally turns scarlet in autumn but is more likely to be seen at this time with leaves of yellow or orange *left*.

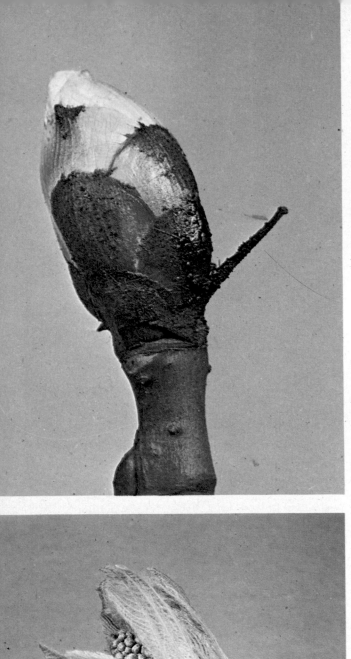

52

The Horse Chestnut

The Horse Chestnut is a popular ornamental tree which grows to a majestic domed shape *below*. It produces "sticky buds" which obligingly open when placed in water indoors *left*, has unique tall "candles" of flowers (a potential flower head is shown *bottom near left*) and produces the conkers *right* collected by small boys wherever the tree is found. In Turkey, its native country, the "nuts" were fed to ailing horses but animals normally refuse to eat them.

Gum Trees

Most of the 500 species of Eucalyptus or Gum trees come from Australia and grow in a wide range of habitats. The one sometimes called White Sally *below* grows in the mountains; the common Red River Gums *right* grow along rivers and watercourses. The foliage of the gum tree is unusual because the juvenile true leaves are often differently shaped from the leaves of the adult tree. The flower bud looks like a little urn with a lid which is pushed off as the stamens inside expand. The lids have already come off in this illustration of the Red-flowered Gum *left*.

Dogwood

The Dogwood family is a small one consisting mostly of shrubs and small trees. All have very small flowers, which seems a contradictory statement, for the glory of a Flowering Dogwood in bloom *left* and of the blossom *below* implies that the flowers are in fact large. This mass of colour is, however, due to large white or pinkish bracts, modified leaves which protect the developing flowers and provide part of the attraction for insect pollinators. Dogwood trees in flower in spring are nearly as much of an attraction as the fall colours in New England, and rightly so. In autumn the foliage of Dogwood trees is very colourful and in addition the trees are covered with bunches of bright red berries at this time. The Cornelian Cherry is a European species of Dogwood; the berries *right* are typical of the genus. The small yellow flowers of this plant are slightly larger than those of the Flowering Dogwood but look smaller as they do not have coloured bracts. They still show up well though as they appear on bare twigs in winter and very early spring. The wood of Dogwood trees is hard and very strong and was used for small items that needed to be tough like skewers and wheel hubs.

The Bignonia Family

The bignonia family is largely made up of tropical and subtropical species which come mainly from South America; only a few are native to temperate regions. The five-lobed flower is typically funnel-shaped and bisexual; there are only four stamens, two long and two short. The Sausage Tree is the only species of this family native to tropical Africa and is so called because of its long sausage-like fruits *left*. The flowers open in the evening, emitting a mouse-like smell which attracts bats who come to feed on

pollen and nectar, pollinating them in the process. These newly-opened flowers have fallen by the next morning. There are about fifty species of Jacaranda *below left*, two or three of which are commonly grown as street trees in tropical towns and cities.

The large flowers of the African Tulip Tree *right* are typical of the family and are particularly conspicuous because they project above the leafy bulk of the tree. Those of the Indian Bean Tree *(Catalpa) below* are similar, if more foxglove-like; the very big leaves are heart-shaped and the pods are long, measuring up to forty centimetres. This tree is found in the wild only in North America and China.

The Bombax Family

The tropical trees which comprise the bombax family are related to the cacao and allied to the mallows. Most have large and showy flowers like these of *Bombax ellipticum, right,* and its near relative the Silk Cotton Tree *(B. ceiba) below.* The Baobab must be the best known of all this family. It has a trunk with a girth larger than that of any other tree, the diameter can be more than eight metres; this trunk is sometimes excavated to form a human dwelling. Arabian legend has it that "the devil plucked up the baobab, thrust its branches into the earth and left its roots in the air". It certainly is a very odd-looking tree; in the foreground *left* a tree has been broken down by elephants, probably while trying to get at the juicy interior during conditions of drought, and there is a living tree behind. The picture gives an idea of the fibrous nature of the wood, the bark fibres of which are sometimes used to make rope or cloth. Pollination by bats is widespread in this family and the Baobab is no exception. It has rather drab flowers whose numerous stamens hang down below the leaves where they brush on bats visiting the flowers for nectar.

Palms

The Palms look rather different from the other flowering trees and they are indeed different botanically in that they are monocotyledons not dicotyledons, having one seed leaf not two. Typically they have a single trunk without branches which, because it lacks cambium, grows taller without growing thicker. The Doum Palms of Kenya *left* are atypical in that they have freely-branched stems. The palm trunk is soft and pithy and is surrounded by corky or fibrous tissue. The leaves can be huge, some reaching a length of as much as five metres; the wind-pollinated flowers are frequently large too. Most palms will only thrive in the tropics where they are particularly valuable as they will live in conditions of heat and drought that no other plants can endure. They are economically important – the Coconut Palm is the most widely distributed of all the tropical trees – and provide raffia, betel nuts, palm wine, palm sugar, palm oil and dates as well as coconuts. Palms can be very decorative in the wild as are these *Mauritia flexuosa* growing in the coastal swamp of Guyana *left* and the scarlet-trunked Sealing Wax Palms from the Pacific Islands *right*.

INDEX

Page numbers refer to illustrations.

First published in Great Britain 1978 by Colour Library International Ltd.,
Designed by David Gibbon. Produced by Ted Smart.
© Text: Jacqueline Seymour © Illustrations CLI/Bruce Coleman Ltd.
Colour separations by La Cromolito, Milan, Italy.
Display and Text filmsetting by Focus Photoset, London, England.
Printed by I.G. Domingo and bound by Eurobinder, Barcelona (Spain)
All rights reserved.
ISBN No. 0 904681 44 0
COOMBE BOOKS